Three Strikes, but Not Out

✝ by Dr. Marion Jones ✝

To Shirlynn,
I'm praying that God's
total will, will be done
in your life.
Love Pastor

DORRANCE PUBLISHING CO., INC.
PITTSBURGH, PENNSYLVANIA 15222

ISBN # 0-8059-4533-4
Printed in the United States of America

First Printing

For information or to order additional books, please write:
Dorrance Publishing Co., Inc.
643 Smithfield Street
Pittsburgh, Pennsylvania 15222
U.S.A.

Dedication

I dedicate this book to my husband James Waddell Jones,
my closest friend for more than thirty-eight years
of marriage and ministry,
with whom I have shared so much through the years.

I feel he is of a special breed,
to be able to deal with a wife who is in the public eye,
and whose time and energy is often spent with others.

Thanks, "Honey," for your understanding and love.

Special thanks to the St. Mark Church of Deliverance family,
for putting up with me, and allowing me to obey the will of God,
and to follow the vision that He has given.

I want to pay special tribute to my children, Ronald, James, Anthony,
Carla, and Christopher, for their support and prayers.

Contents

Introduction

During the latter part of 1993, I was inspired by the Holy Spirit to write this book. As a female in ministry, I desire to encourage and inspire women who are faithful to the call of God to preach the Gospel. I believe that I was brought to the kingdom for such a time as this.

In the beginning of my ministry, God let me know that He had made me a prophet to the nations—to help build the body of Christ, to root up, to tear down, to rebuild, and to plant. In the past twenty years, we have seen the power of God manifested in these areas, and souls have been set free.

I thank God for the privilege of sharing with you the miracles that He has performed in my life and ministry; of sharing with you how God used those things that were meant for harm, and made them to be a blessing and a source of maturity. Through them I've learned "oppositions are doors of opportunity." God will take those things that are meant for evil to prove Himself to those who love Him, and are the called according to His purpose. (Rom. 8:28)

I trust that this will be a source of encouragement, especially to the women who are in the ministry who find themselves in the midst of great opposition as they are striving to do the will of God. I am glad that these words were written in the Holy Scriptures: "For ye see your calling brethren, how that not many wise men after the flesh, not many mighty, not many noble, are called: But God hath chosen the foolish things of the world to confound the wise; and God hath chosen the weak things of the world to confound the things which are mighty; And base things of the world and things which are despised, hath God chosen, yea, and things which are not, to bring to nought things that are: That no flesh should glory in his presence." (1 Cor. 1:26–29) What a word of encouragement to those who feel the least of them all. You may be weak, foolish (according to the world), and base, but thank God we can be, and are, used by God.

Twenty-six years ago I had a visitation from the Holy Spirit. It was at this time God revealed to me His will for my life. I was charged by God to be the pastor of the St. Mark Church of Deliverance. This was later confirmed by Bishop E.D. Brockington of Washington, D.C., who was the presiding Bishop of the Gray's Temple Church of Deliverance in Hampton, Virginia.

One day while in prayer, God began to speak to me. He said, "You have three strikes against you before you get started: (1) you are a woman, (2) your age [I was thirty years old], and (3) your past [I had a child out of wedlock]."

I am grateful for serving a God that will not let you go into anything without warning or instruction. This warning and instruction from God let me know from the beginning that the going would be rough.

In the game of baseball, the batter is allowed to have three strikes before he is called "out." God let me know that I had three strikes against me in life, but in Him I am not "out"!

After I was installed as pastor, I had many battles from within (those who fought against me because of jealousy, and felt that it was not the will of God), and from without. The battle was so strong at one point that I went to God and asked Him to please give this work to my husband. I told God I would work with him with all my might.

God allowed me to pray this way for a while, and then He came to me with the answer from His Word, "Woe unto him that striveth with his Maker!" (Isa. 45:9, 10) "Nay but, O man, who art thou that repliest against God? Shall the thing formed say to Him that formed it, Why hast thou made me thus?" (Rom. 9:20)

I was informed of the fact that He knew my husband and He knew me. His will was done when He called me, and I was transgressing against Him in asking him to choose another. I repented that night and asked Him to forgive me and to strengthen me to do the job He had called me to do. Pastoring is not an easy task, and it is even more difficult when you are a female. But I must confess to you, the good days outweigh the bad.

I wish I could say that every woman in ministry has been a compliment to ministry, but I cannot. Some are there for the wrong reasons. They have been hurt by those who did not understand the call of God upon their lives, and now they are bitter and angry, or feel they have something to prove.

Then there are those who are in ministry totally because of God's will for them. Those women had been comfortable helping and supporting, but God spoke to them through times of fasting and prayer concerning His will for their lives. Because of this, my friend, we have nothing to prove. We can say, as Jesus said, "But if I do, though ye believe not me, believe the works." (John 10:38)

Times are changing, yet there are those who are fighting the female in ministry by saying what God has or has not done. I would say to them, souls are dying, men are perishing. We need to stop fighting among ourselves and preach the words of life to those in need, that they might be saved, healed, and delivered, and leave the other matters with God. He is the one to judge whether He did or did not.

The Formative Years

✟ Chapter 1 ✟

Like the prophet Jeremiah, I heard God speak down in my spirit, *"Before I formed thee in the belly I knew thee; and before thou camest forth out of the womb I sanctified thee, and I ordained thee a prophet unto the nations."* (Jer. 1:5)

At an early age I felt a tugging in my heart for God. I could not explain it, but it was there. You know how that is? You feel something going on within you that you don't understand, but you know it's real.

In 1948, all the lights of the city went out, and they remained out for some time. It was what they called a "blackout." I learned later it was a safety drill to protect us from the threat of bombing. I don't know whether it was the real thing or a test.

The night of the blackout someone was going through the streets shouting, "It's judgment day!" I was about nine years old at the time, and I remember thinking, *What would happen to me if this were judgment day; would I go to heaven?*

I can't remember whether or not I had heard anything about God at that point in my life. There had not been any teaching about God from my mother. My grandmother was the only one I knew who went to church. Neither my mother nor my immediate family were religious. The only memory I have of my mother relative to God at that time was the night a few women from the Holiness Church came to the house for prayer.

Mother Carrie Johnson and others came that night. My sisters were asleep at the time, but I could not sleep. It seemed to me I was drawn to the living room where they were in prayer. I stood in the hallway and peeped around the corner to see what was happening. I saw my mother laying prostrate on the floor and the women praying for her. I did not know what it was all about, but I wanted so much to go in there. I watched with the curiosity of a child, wondering what was happening to my mother. I was not frightened, I just wanted it to happen to me.

From that night, a hunger for God was stirred in me. I didn't understand it at all, but I knew it was about God. After that time I never saw my mother seeking God (at this time she is saved, praise God, and a faithful member of my church).

My grandmother, Minnie Heath, a devout Christian, began to come to the house and take me to church. I loved going to church. I was so excited when she would come to pick me up. Granny was a member of the choir at her church. She would sing the songs of praise to God and would shout in the process. I thank God that she was concerned enough to take me to the church so I could get to know God.

As I continued to go to church with my grandmother, I would sit in the service and a longing came to me for greater experience in the Lord. I was young, but I felt that there was a greater depth in God than what I experienced when I went to church with my grandmother. At that time I did not realize what it was because I was not born-again.

I desired to feel the joy of the Lord when I went to church. I didn't feel Him, and it bothered me. I began to say in my heart as a child, "I don't like this kind of service." I had never seen people shout and praise God like I was feeling, but I knew what I felt. That is why I tell the people in the church to leave the children alone when they begin to praise the Lord in the service, because you don't know how God is moving upon them.

Life Changed

✟ Chapter 2 ✟

A few years later my family moved from Fifty-second Street in Newport News, to Forty-eighth Street. The house we lived in on Fifty-second Street was a very nice apartment. It was well kept. My mother was an immaculate housekeeper. I tell everyone that her house was so clean, you could have eaten off her floors. The landlord had maintained those apartments, and they were in excellent condition. As I remember, they were like new.

When we moved to Forty-eighth Street, my mother was very upset because the condition of those apartments was nothing like the ones we had left. They were dirty, and the walls seemed to have never had any paint on them. They were also smelly. This was very frustrating to my mother, but it was the area in which my stepfather wanted to live. Looking back, I can see it was God's will for me.

The apartment we lived in was a duplex type of housing. Deacon Herbert Thorne and his wife Juanita lived there. The Thornes were members of Gray's Temple Church of Deliverance, where Bishop P.B. Gray was the pastor. This is the place where my life was changed.

One Monday afternoon I was walking around the two-family complex when I heard voices coming from the bedroom area of the Thornes' apartment. The sound was prayer, and it drew me inside. The Lord had it so that they had not locked the door. When I got inside, the saints were on their knees praying. Automatically I bowed.

When they discovered I was there, they came over to me and asked if I wanted to accept the Lord. I said, "Yes." They prayed with me, and that day I received Jesus as my Savior. I could tell that a distinct change had taken place in me.

When the prayer was over and I went outside, everything about me was different and new. The sun seemed to be brighter. I began to look to the ground because it seemed that I was floating. There was an ant on the ground and I stepped over it because I did not want to kill it. There was so much of the love of God in my heart, I did not want to hurt anything.

Some people say you don't necessarily feel anything when you accept Jesus in your heart, but I beg to differ with them. You feel a change in yourself. No, we don't go by feelings, but you know that there is a definite change. There is a song they used to sing when I was young in the Lord: "There is a new change in me, a new change in me, I am so happy I am so free. Since Jesus came into my life . . . . Oh, oh, oh, a new change in me." You don't hear that very often now, but I believe that song was written by someone who had a definite experience.

The children who were outside began to tease me when I came out and said, "Marion, we heard you in there." It didn't matter to me that they heard me; a change had taken place. I walked about that day so joyful and happy in my heart and soul. At that time I was eleven years old, and I can remember it as though it were today.

In the house praying that day were Sister Juanita Thorne, Sister Catharine Matthews (whom God used to help me in the ways of the Lord), and Mother Edith Gray (my former pastor).

Sister Catharine Matthews adopted me as her spiritual daughter. She had no children of her own, and she was not married at the time. She was God's instrument in those formative years to keep me encouraged, because no one else in my family had been saved. Sister Matthews saw to it that I stayed in the church. I remember the days she and I would walk to church. We were members of the St. John Church of God Live On; Elder John A. Stephenson was the pastor.

She would talk to me and instruct me in the ways of the Lord. We didn't have a car, so we walked from Forty-eighth Street to Roanoke Avenue to church most of the time. Someone would bring us back home at night due to the dangers women face walking alone late at night.

Mother Matthews took me everywhere she went. Through her motherly care and Godly concern, I was given the opportunity to travel from state to state, and from city to city in fellowship with other young people in the church. Oh! If mothers in Zion would do that now. So many young people need the aid of mothers and fathers in the church—those that will reach out a helping hand to them. Some are in homes where there is no one saved but them. That is a difficult thing, and they need the encouragement of others to help them.

Mother Matthews has gone on to be with the Lord, but I will never forget her love for me. I pray that God will move upon others in the church to adopt some young person, and be that mother or father to them. You never know who you are nurturing.

Satan's Plan of Destruction

✞ Chapter 3 ✞

"The thief cometh not, but for to steal, and to kill, and to destroy: I am come that they might have life, and that they have it more abundantly." (John 10:10)

All went well for about five years. When I became a teenager, changes began to take place. It began with sexual abuse from my stepfather. I remember the nights of harassment when he was home. My stepfather was a merchant seaman, and many times he was not home. My mother basically raised her children alone.

He would come into my room at night when everyone was asleep. I was terrified. At that time things were not the way they are now. Children are taught in school and at home that if someone touches you in an area of your body that you don't feel comfortable with, to tell someone.

I believe that if it had been that way then, I would have revealed it to someone. But I thought it was my fault, and if I talked they would blame me for it. So I held my peace as many do when they are abused, and lived in fear night and day.

This abuse went on for about two years. From that point, my life took an awful turn. I still loved God, but I could not deal with the desires that were aroused in me and the guilt I lived with because of it. I began to keep company with the wrong people (those who were not saved) in school. They were good young people, but they were not born-again.

This caused me to go farther and farther away from the will of God, and to yield more to the desires of the flesh. I blame no one by myself for what happened to me. I did not pray as I should have. I did not fast to keep this body under subjection to the will of God.

At the age of fifteen, I became pregnant. This was a devastating thing for me. I believe it was the plan of Satan to destroy me. After I discovered that I was pregnant, Satan came to me one night and said, "Now that you are pregnant, kill yourself. Walk out into the middle of the highway (which was near our house) and let a car hit you." Because of the guilt I felt, I obeyed Satan.

I walked out toward the highway that night. I was so depressed in my mind and spirit at that time, I was ready to end my life. While I was walking toward the street, I heard this voice say to me, "Go back into the house!" I didn't know then, but I know now, it was the angel of the Lord. He was sent by God to stop me from killing myself and my child.

If Satan had had his way, my son and I would have been killed, and neither of us would have had the opportunity to do that which God had foreordained for us. I believe that what Satan had planned for our destruction, God, even in the midst of disobedience, turned and made it work together for our good.

Months later, my son Ronald, whom I love dearly, was born. I wish I could say that all went well after his birth, but it did not. It seemed to continue to get worse. Due to the circumstances surrounding my life and family at that time (at this point I will not go into details, because I am not writing this to hurt those I love, but only to show the hand of God in my life), I lost Ronald, not in death, but to another family.

Satan wanted to use this also to destroy me, but God was with me. In the midst of turmoil in the home, I made an unwise decision—I let my son go. After a short time I realized my mistake. I suffered days and nights of pain desiring to have my son back, to no avail. I thought the pain would never end. When I sought to rectify the problem it was (I thought) too late.

I was denied the privilege of caring for and raising my son. When you are young there are many things you don't know concerning the law or your rights as a person. Had I known what I know now, **I would have fought to the bitter end for him.**

Shortly after that time, I married my husband, James Waddell Jones. He was a nice young man from Spring Lake, North Carolina. I thank God for "Jones," because through him I received much help and consolation during that difficult time. I met Jones when Ron was about three or four months old. It seemed he fell in love with Ron from the beginning. Had I listened to him, I would have never suffered that anguish. I allowed what I was going through to block out sound reasoning. Jones has always loved Ron, and wanted him for his son.

I suffered years of pain and agony from this situation until one day I said to God, "I can't live like this; please take this out of my heart. Not my son, but the torment of not having him."

God was faithful, and He helped me. He lifted the torment from my thoughts and gave me peace of mind as I waited upon Him to work it all out. And work it out He did! Years passed and one day God gave me my son, after I was told I would never have him again. Oh! God is faithful. If you have the patience to wait on Him, He will come, and He will deliver! Praise God!

———

Today Ron is pastoring a beautiful church in Chattanooga, Tennessee. He has a wonderful group of people, and God is yet giving the increase. I thank God for Ron's wife Deborah, and her mother, Elect Davis. They are the instruments God used to bring my son to me. Elect Lady Davis is the pastor of a great church in North Carolina. To God be the glory for each of them for allowing Him to bring about this miracle.

Answering the Call

✟ Chapter 4 ✟

"Also I heard the voice of the Lord saying, Whom shall I send, and who will go for us? Then I said, Here am I; send me."
(Isa. 6:8)

In 1957, at the age of eighteen years, I preached my first initial message. I was under the leadership of Elder Samuel Braxton, at the Holy Tabernacle in Denbigh, Virginia. My first message was "The Great Deliverer." The message was based upon the life and purpose of Jesus Christ, Who came to this earth to deliver man from the powers of Satan, and to bring them into the kingdom of God.

I ministered like any young person would who was not very familiar with her new position. In other words, I was nervous. God is faithful, and He carried me through and blessed those who were there. I thank God for those who encouraged me during that time—those who God gave to witness His call upon my life. I was a diamond in the rough that needed to be worked on and brought to its fullest potential.

Thank God for the years of experience He has given me: years of fasting and prayer; time in His presence; seeking to know him, and to receive direction from him; and days when nothing mattered but him. I was, as the Psalm says, "As the hart panteth for the water brook, so my soul longest after thee, O God." (Ps. 42:1)

God dealt with me daily through His Word, fasting, and prayer. As I studied His Word I was inspired by the Spirit to underline the passages of the Holy Scripture given to me. After much time had elapsed, I was led by the Holy Spirit to go to the Bible and read all the Scriptures He had given. When I did they all pointed to the ministry of Jesus Christ—the ministry of deliverance. Luke 4:18 reads, "The Spirit of the Lord is upon me, because he hath anointed me to preach the Gospel to the poor; he hath sent me to heal the brokenhearted, to preach deliverance to the captives, and recovering of sight to the blind, to set at liberty them that are bruised . . . ."

At that time God let me known that this was the type of ministry He had given to me. I thank God for His faithfulness. Through years of fasting, prayer, and the study of His Word, the revelation of Jesus Christ has come to me. He has made Himself known to me.

The tests and the trials have been teachers, because through them I have experienced the love, power, and the faithfulness of my God. I have learned that He is true to His Word. What He says, He will do. Not one word will fall to the ground. "They will not return to Him void, but they will accomplish what he sent it to." (Isa. 55:11)

Though hell come out against it, Jesus said, "The gates of hell shall not prevail." (Matt. 16:18) I remember the song that says, "You can't make me doubt him, you can't make me doubt him, you can't make me doubt him in my heart. You can't make me doubt him, I know too much about him . . . . "

Through his Word, and by His Spirit, He has made me to know Him. A person with an experience beats a man with an argument every time. I heard God say to me in noonday prayer, "They have an argument, but you have an experience. You have it because I gave it to you." Truly he has made me to know him!

God brought me from sexual abuse, fear, and deep frustration. I remember the times my mother's house was broken into. The first time it happened, I was not home; I was at church. I came home late that night, and knocked on the door for someone to let me in. My mother came to the door looking very strange. When I asked her what was wrong, she told me someone had broken into the house, and when they heard me at the door they fled.

This happened several times, and each time God allowed me to come to the rescue of my mother. One of the times the house was broken into I was home and in bed asleep like the others in the family. I heard screaming and a big commotion in my mother's room. At first I thought I was dreaming, because when I awakened all was dark. This was not the way she went to sleep. Because of previous intrusions, my mother would leave a light on so we would not be in the dark. I dosed off, and again I heard bumping and screaming. I raised up in the bed that I shared with two sisters, and listened attentively, and then I realized it was my mother.

I jumped up from the bed, and without any thought of danger to myself, I ran to the aid of my mother. There in the darkness she was struggling with a young man who we found out later was Linwood Bunch. Mr. Bunch had broken into other homes and had raped women who were alone.

I began to assist my mother in her struggle with this man. He was so strong that he pulled my mother and me out the door. When we came back into the house there was a stick leaning against the wall. Oh! How I wished I had known it was there before; I would have used it to crack his head.

I looked at my mother when I turned the lights on, and her face was bloody and swollen. He had beaten her for not yielding to him. This made me very angry. I am grateful to God that he did not kill my mother. Mr. Bunch was tried later for raping other women, and he received the electric chair for his crime.

Due to the circumstances and situation that I went through, I became fearful. I was afraid of my shadow. I ran from the least noise, the least unusual sight. I remember coming home one night from the drugstore, where I had gone to get a snack and a book to read. Looking up into the sky there was a light—the type used to advertise new businesses and so forth.

I did not know what it was and **I ran like crazy.** Between the house and the drugstore was a ditch. I jumped that ditch like it was nothing, and I ran home. Fear is an awful thing to have. It is torment. You cannot rest night or day. You are always looking behind you, or looking under beds and other places when you have fear.

I was so fearful that my voice had a soprano pitch to it. I talked in soprano. God used Elder Samuel Braxton Sr. while on a ten day and night fast to minister to me, and deliver me from that tormenting force of Satan. My friend, you may be suffering today from fear. I want to pray for all of you who are being tormented with this same spirit. The same God that delivered me will deliver you. He is no respecter of persons. Come on, let's believe God and release your faith in Him. IN THE NAME OF JESUS, I COMMAND THE SPIRIT OF FEAR TO LOOSE YOU. SATAN I ADJURE YOU IN THE NAME OF JESUS, COME OUT! BE GONE, NOW! Receive it now, my friend, and Jesus will make you WHOLE! AMEN.

In 1965, in noonday prayer, God led Elder Edith Gray (wife of Bishop P.B. Gray, my pastor at the time) to come to Portsmouth to reestablish the church that had been organized years before, but was at that time inactive. Several ministers had been sent to pastor the church, but none remained.

When Elder Edith Gray told us what God had spoken to her, I felt led to accompany her. With the permission of my pastor and Bishop, I came to help. God instructed her to come certain days for prayer. After prayer we would go from house to house telling the neighbors about Jesus Christ.

God blessed our obedience, and souls were saved. Those who had backslidden from God were reclaimed. Oppressed were set free. Bodies were healed by the power of God.

We started in a one-room building that had no running water or a rest room. We had to go to the neighbors for assistance, or wait when we had need.

I had one child and was carrying another, but I wanted to be obedient to the call of God. Coming from Hampton week after week in that condition was not easy. It was very trying at times, but I knew it was God's will for me. I never had the slightest idea that God was preparing me for leadership. I worked faithfully with my pastor, fasting and praying that God's will would be done in that branch of Zion.

We remained in that building, and in that type of situation, for about a year. After that God blessed us to move to a regular church building, which was owned by Bishop King David Johnson, in Carrolton, Virginia, 1230 Graham Street, in Ports. The ministry expanded. Souls were added to the church. Pastor Gray gave me several responsibilities. I was made the youth leader, the director of the choir, musician for the service, and at a later date I became one of the van drivers to transport the people to church.

My hands were full, for by this time I had four children, a husband to care for, and a house to keep. God was faithful; he gave me the strength to do them all. Many days I was so exhausted, and wondered why I had to do this. Why did I have to go so far to church?

I looked at my friends who attended church in Hampton and Newport News, and said to God, "Why can't I go to church over here?" Night after night, mile after mile, it was not easy, but it was His will for me. You see, He had a plan, and He was getting me ready for it.

Elder Edith Gray was one of the greatest women preachers I had ever heard. The anointing of the Holy Ghost was heavy upon her. She was my mentor. I was deeply impressed with her love and devotion to God. She was a woman of consecration and great faith who taught us to believe and trust God in all things.

When we were going through our test, and it seemed like things were bad, she would say to us, "You don't worry about anything but pleasing God. And when you please Him, He will make your enemies to be at peace with you."

Mother (as we called her) was a friend and teacher. She was a prophet of God. We watched the words that came from her lips, and we saw them come to pass. She was endowed with the Spirit of discernment. She could look at you and could see (it seemed) through you. God walked heavy in her life. She had some relationship with Him.

I worked with her for seven years, and was trained to believe, trust, obey, and love the Lord. She did not preach one thing and live another. What she preached, we saw her live. Mother was an example to us of dedication, devotion, and consecration. I am so grateful to God for giving me such a leader—one I could look up to and follow, as she followed Christ.

When God took her home to be with Him, I was deeply grieved. I was devoted to her and the vision God gave her. I felt that I did not want to live any longer, I loved her so much. I had such respect for her as the servant of God. The day of her home going service I thought I would die. *God! What am I going to do now?* I thank God for the saints who came and encouraged me that day. Through their encouragement I was able to stand up and pray to God for help to deal.

I miss Mother Gray so much, but I am determined to live the word that she preached to us; to be an example of that strength and dedication so greatly displayed through her.

After her death I continued praying with the church, waiting for God to give us a pastor. One day shortly afterward God began to deal with me about pastoring the church. I wept. This weeping lasted for a month. I didn't want the position. I prayed to God and I explained (smile) to Him, I did not want to pastor. Most of the adult people at the church were older than I was. They were not going to receive me as their pastor. This was a somber time of weeping. I was heartbroken about it.

God allowed me to share my heart, and when the time had come He said to me on my job (I was working at this time), "It's time for you to stop crying now, and go forward." I had always told my pastor that is one job I would never have. I observed the hardships and persecutions that she suffered, and I wanted no part of it. I remember the time someone stood before us one Sunday and spoke in such an insolent way to her. I watched to see what she would do about it, and she did nothing.

This person pointed her finger in my pastor's face and spoke her peace. This made me angry. I wanted her to say something or do something, but she only smiled and bore it. On the way home I talked to her about it. I said to her, "You let her do that to you and you did nothing. I just couldn't be a pastor." She only looked at me and smiled. Later she said, "You don't know what God is doing to do with you." I said, "I will never be a pastor!"

I have suffered things similar and even worse. You have the heart of Jesus Christ when you are called to lead. You deal like He would in situations. You want to be pleasing to God in your dealing. He equips you to handle it, Amen!

Pastoral Years

✟ Chapter 5 ✟

"And I will give you pastors according to mine heart, which shall feed you with knowledge and understanding."
(Jer. 3:15)

I began pastoring in 1969, after the death of my pastor, Elder Edith Gray. There were those who did not agree because of my age. They said I was too young and had too many children (four), but God always has the final say.

We remained in the church on Graham Street for about one year. Toward the end of the year I had a dream. I saw the membership assembled for worship and in walked Bishop K.D. Johnson (the owner of the building). He said to me, "You've got to leave. I have someone else to place in the church." In the dream the members were very upset. Some were crying about it.

The next time I went to church for the service I told the people about the dream. I told them that I did not want them to grieve about it because the Lord was with us, and He would give us a place.

That Sunday evening after we had eaten our dinner, Bishop K.D. Johnson came over to the church, and the words I heard him speak to me in the dream were said to me that day. I told him that I had seen him say those words to me a few days before in a dream. He was astonished.

His suggestion to me was, "Go and find yourself a storefront somewhere." I said to him, "God is going to give us a building to worship in, and it's not going to be a storefront either." The words that came out of my mouth were words of faith. I had no idea where we would go, but I felt this very strongly.

The days that followed were trying times indeed for the church, and for me as a young pastor. We went from place to place trying to find a building in which to worship. Bishop Johnson gave us thirty days to relocate. That time went by so quickly. Toward the end of the allotted time God used Minister Janie Carter (my assistant pastor at that time) to contact the people at the Lodge building on Elm Street. They allowed us to have service there on Sundays.

After a short time, we were asked to leave because they said we were too noisy in our worship. When this happened, we were directed to the original building that had been used years ago by a minister who had worked under my Bishop (P.B. Gray) on Virginia Avenue.

It was a two-story house that was converted into a church. Downstairs was the sanctuary, and upstairs was an apartment. The building was deteriorating, and we worked hard to bring it up to an acceptable standard. Bishop E.D. Brockington (our Bishop at that time) and some of the men from the fellowship churches came over and gave their service to help us.

Many changes had to be made, and God blessed them to do it. This building was smaller than the church we had to move out of on Graham Street, so we had growing pains. I sought the Lord as to the next step. *"Should we make plans to build there on Virginia Avenue, or what should we do?"* I stayed before Him until it was made clear.

While we waited on God, I looked into the matter as to whether or not we could build a new church in the area where the house was located. We went to the city to seek the answer. We learned the property we were worshipping on was residential property. In order to build a church, it had to be re-zoned to commercial. Well, we went into spiritual warfare. We prayed, and God gave us the victory.

I shared this incident with you to let you know that while you are waiting on God, you should put your faith to work. Don't sit still and wait for it all to drop down to you. You do what you know how to do, and God will take care of what you can't do.

We stayed on Virginia Avenue for two years. During that time I invited Evangelist Edith Byrd (the cousin of my pastor) to come and conduct revival for us. She came and God used her to speak prophetic words to us. One night in the revival, God spoke through her and asked us, "Who can believe that God can bring that that's out of sight into sight?"

Immediately I had an open-eyed vision. The building we now worship in came before me on what seemed to be a large movie screen. I jumped to my feet and shouted, "Yes, I do!" After service the next day, I shared the vision with her, and the desire we had to purchase the property. She agreed with us in faith, and we went the next day to "spy out the land."

By a miraculous intervention of God, Deaconess Sybil Herbert and Minister Janie Carter found the owner of the property, Mr. Goodman, at 615 Washington Street, and the Lord did the rest! I get excited even today when I remember how God manifested His power and favor to us.

The building was not advertised, but God allowed us to get the information necessary to talk to Mr. Goodman. From day one, I saw God had given us favor with him. He gave us the key to look at the church. We went inside. You know how it is when you know what you know you know? Praise God!

The church was complete with robes, china in the kitchen, and silver-ware in the drawers. When I came outside I said, "God, I stand on your word that says 'every foot of ground that you tread upon, I have given it to you'." (Deut. 11:24, 25)

I was not familiar with business dealings, so I prayed for the direction of the Lord. He led me to contact Bishop L.E. Willis, Bishop of the New Frontier Church of God in Christ in Portsmouth, Virginia. Bishop gave me sound advice. I followed his instructions, and God blessed it.

After several visits with Mr. Goodman, we asked him for a binding contract because others were interested in the property, and had the mon-eys to buy it. They were even willing to pay more for it, but God moved upon Mr. Goodman to dictate a statement to his secretary. After she fin-ished he had her read it to us. She read the statement three times, because we were listening for the words "binding contract" and we did not hear it.

Mr. Goodman said to me, "Reverend Jones, listen again." When she finished that time he said to me, "This is better than a binding contract; this is a bill of sale." Praise God! Without a penny down we were given a bill of sale. Mr. Goodman then asked me, "How much do you think you can pay for mortgage?" He did not accept the amount that I offered him. So I asked him to suggest an amount, and as God had it, he only asked for one hun-dred dollars more than my offer. This amount was large for us because of the size of our congregation.

By faith I said to him, "We can handle it." I had no idea how we would do it, but I know God said, "I have given it to you!" We were given the liberty to go into the building and have revival, and we have been having revival ever since. When God says something, regardless of what you have to face, His words will come to pass. When He speaks, the power to per-form it comes with His Word.

No devil in hell can prevent God's Word from being performed in your life. All He asks you to do is believe, and trust Him. He is a God of His Word. When you know that God has spoken to you, walk out on His Word. He said, "Heaven and earth shall pass away, but my Word will not pass away. Not one jot or tittle . . . . (Matt. 5:18) That impossible thing you have before Him, believe and it shall come to pass. Amen! We are as of this year, 1995, making plans to expand. God has blessed us to pay for the building, and we are now getting ready to add to it. To God be all the glory!

Radio Ministry

✟ Chapter 6 ✟

"Go ye therefore, and teach all nations . . . ."
(Matt. 28:10)

"And the Lord said unto the servant, Go out into the highways and hedges, and compel them to come in, that my house may be filled."
(Luke 14:23)

After a few years of pastoring, God began to deal with me about the radio ministry. Evangelist Ralph Nickols from New York came to Norfolk for a crusade. I was led by the Lord to attend. Ralph Nickols had been recently installed as pastor of the church and ministry that Apostle A. Skinner had founded.

The night I attended the crusade, I did not feel well, but I went. The man of God preached a great message as to the power of God, and His willingness to heal and deliver all who needed the help of the Lord. After he finished preaching, he made an altar call for all who needed the power of God to save, heal, and deliver. I had such a tremendous headache, I thought my head would burst.

When I stood before him, he said nothing about healing. God began to use him in the gift of the word of knowledge. He said, "I don't know who you are, but I see God using your voice to deliver many. God is going to use your voice."

I left there that night wondering how this would be. I was already preaching, how else could God use my voice? I was reminded of a vision I had years before I became pastor. I saw myself standing on the side of the highway preaching the Word of God. I was shouting, "For God so loved the world that He gave his only begotten Son, that whosoever believeth in him, shall not perish, but shall have everlasting life!"

While I was preaching, cars were zooming past me. When I awakened, I said, "God, what was I doing standing on the side of the road preaching to swiftly moving cars?" I went to my pastor and shared the vision with her. She said it was God, but it was not for then; it would be in time to come.

God said to me in prayer, "What I was showing you was the radio ministry. I am going to use you in that capacity." He sent his servant years later to confirm what He had shown me.

In noonday prayer I was visited by God again about the radio ministry. I was praying and saw another vision. As I laid on the floor in the presence of God, I saw people who were caught in a large net. I looked again and I saw some bound with large chains about their ankles. God began to explain this sight to me. He said, "My people are bound, some because of what they have done, and others by the will of man. But I'm going to use you to set them free."

I sought the Lord as to a name for the broadcast, and He said to me, "Use the title, 'Words of Spirit and Life'." He gave me the Scripture to back up what He spoke to me (John 6:63), "It is the Spirit that quickeneth; the flesh profiteth nothing: the words that I speak unto you, they are Spirit, and they are life."

Souls have been saved, bodies have been healed, families restored. God's people have received help and deliverance.

One day as I was changing classes on the campus of Norfolk State University, a young lady came up to me and said, "Reverend Jones, you don't know me, but I want you to know I was a dope addict." You could see upon her continuance that she had been heavily addicted. She continued, "I began to listen to your broadcast and God saved me. I didn't know how to deal with the test I was going through after giving my heart to the Lord. But as I continued to listen to you teach, I was instructed as to how to go through my test. I have learned how to keep the victory."

Oh! What a blessing to hear that testimony. There have been many, many more, but it is worth it just for that one soul. Many have come to me personally, in department stores, grocery stores, drugstores, and wherever I am, and said, "You are such a blessing. I have learned how to go through the test, how to believe in God in impossible situations, and how to stand on the Word of God." Some have said, "How can you know what to preach? You preached right to me today, yesterday, and so forth." Many have come to the church from the broadcast saying, "You told me God said, 'Get up from there, He sees you, and He is going to deliver'." I say, "No man can do these things, except God be with him."

God has set the captives free; He has loosed the bound. He has set at liberty those who were bruised. He has saved the lost, and worked many miracles. To God be the glory, great things He has done!

Fiery Trials

✝ Chapter 7 ✝

"Beloved, think it not strange concerning the fiery trial which is to try you, as though some strange thing happened unto you: But rejoice, inasmuch as ye are partakers of Christ's sufferings; that, when his glory shall be revealed, ye may be glad also with exceeding joy."
(1 Pet. 4:12, 13)

God blessed us to move into the building on Washington and County Streets in Portsmouth, Virginia, with the help of the owner, Mr. Goodman. But the move was not without great tests. It would seem that those with whom I was in fellowship would have rejoiced with me, but instead some I thought were friends turned away from me. Reports went out that I was too big now to have anything to do with the small churches.

This kind of report caused me quite a bit of anguish. I knew it was from Satan, nonetheless, it was believed by some. Nothing about me had changed. God had just moved me from one place to another.

I remember the week of the dedication. There I was stretched out in faith. I was moving in a realm of faith that I had not experienced before and I needed all the support I could get. Most of the preachers who came were not encouraging. It was as thought they were preaching *on* me rather than rejoicing *with* me. It was one of the worst weeks I have experienced as a pastor.

I came to the service one night of the dedication, and those who were on the quest that night filled the platform, and did not leave a chair for me to sit in. When I arrived, the pulpit was filled with the brethren in black suits. I would have sat on the floor, but the membership would not have it. When the preacher delivered the message, it was about counting the cost. He read the Scripture from Luke 14:28–30. As he preached, he turned to me and said, "I hope you had as much knowledge as this man did before you began this venture." At that point I didn't need to hear that. I needed to hear someone say to me and the church that nothing is too difficult for the Lord. If you wait on the Lord He will bring you out unconquered.

I had taken this step of faith. I had never taken such a giant step before. I heard God speak to me, and I obeyed Him.

Another came and used the Scripture from 2 Chron. 7:19–22. I love the Word of God. You cannot preach it too straight for me, but when it is preached so as to beat you across the head, you know it. It was as though they wanted me to fail; to fall short of the will of God. I went home each night with great pain in my heart. I said to God, "Can't they see that this is a miracle, and that you have performed this for us?"

God gave me the grace to handle it. It was a painful experience to sit on my platform facing the audience knowing I was the subject of the message. God allowed these things to mature me as a pastor. I never had (thank God) a spirit to fight back. I prayed much, and He fought for me. He manifested His power through me, and His glory was seen.

God has many ways of giving you experiences in Him. Ways of manifesting His power and grace. He said to us, "Think it not strange concerning these fiery trials which is to try you, as though some strange thing happened to you: but rejoice, inasmuch as ye are partakers of Christ's suffering; that when his glory shall be revealed, ye may be glad also with exceeding joy." (1 Pet. 4:12, 13)

The last night of the dedication, Elder Mamie Stephenson, the late pastor of the Triumph Pentecostal Church of Deliverance in Newport News, where the Most Right Reverend Joseph G. Snead is now the pastor and Bishop, came over. God used her in a wonderful way.

Pastor Stephenson said to us that night that God had spoken to her to come and be a blessing to me and the church—and a blessing she was. Words of encouragement came flowing forth from her mouth as she obeyed God. I rejoiced that night to see a true minister of the Gospel stand without jealousy and envy, and speak words to lift up a fellow laborer in the vineyard of the Lord.

Jealousy and greed are two of the reasons we cannot be happy when another is blessed. You must always remember, God is no respecter of persons. What He has done for one, He will do for another, if you are willing to pay the price and step out in faith on His words.

A few years after moving to 615 Washington Street, I remember a gentleman coming to the church. He would stand on the outside and harass the members as they came to church. He would say to them, "You are going to hell for being under this woman pastor." He would tell them to leave the church and go where a male was pastoring. Thank God they knew the Word of God, and were faithful to their church.

I came up to the church one Tuesday for noonday prayer, and there he was. He seemed to be waiting for me to arrive. After I got out of my car and walked around to put coins in the parking meter, he approached me.

He said, "I've been talking to my council about you on this corner. I

19

told them you were doing a good job here, but I know you don't want to go to hell leading these people. They told me to talk to you. Why don't you let a man have this church?"

When I finished putting coins in the meter, I turned to him and said, "You have a good day." I walked off and went into the church and joined the others who had assembled for prayer. I did not have to answer this man. He did not hire me, and, thank God, he could not fire me. I say, as the apostle Peter did when they had commanded them to speak no more in the name of Jesus, " . . . Whether it be right in the sight of God to hearken unto you more than unto God, judge ye. For we cannot but speak the things we have seen and heard." (Acts 4:19, 20)

I thank God for His faithfulness to me. He promised in His Word, the Lord will fight for you and ye shall hold your peace. (Exod. 14:14) We waste precious time and strength fighting for ourselves. There is a greater victory, let God do it! He's better at it than we are.

When God gives you an assignment to carry out for the kingdom, you must remember that all of hell will try to stop your progress. Satan tried Jesus when He came to do the will of the Father. Before He could get to the cross, he tested Him, desiring that He would bow down to him in worship.

My friend, if he tried Jesus, very God, what do you think he will do to you? He never stops. He is always trying to get us to take it back. You know in your spirit that God has spoken to you, but he will strive to make you think it was not God. The devil is a lair! The songwriter said, "Before I take it back, I'll add more to it." Hallelujah! Hallelujah!

I will say this to you: Whenever God speaks to you, He will always give a witness. Whether someone with a relationship with Him, or from the Holy Scriptures, he will never leave Himself without a witness. Stay before Him in prayer. Study the living Word. Have a relationship with Him. When you have a relationship with God, you will have confidence.

"When the enemy shall come in like a flood, the Spirit of the Lord will lift up a standard against him." (Isa. 59:19)

Friends

✝ Chapter 8 ✝

"A friend loveth at all times, and a brother is born for adversity."
(Prov. 17:17)

There are times in ministry when you feel alone. You think, *Lord if there was someone. Someone with whom I could talk, pray, and share the Word of God. Someone with whom I can be myself, and who will not look down on me for what they discover (that I am human like everyone else).*

That feeling of loneliness was so great for me at one time in my ministry, I prayed for God to send me a friend. Now I know that He is a friend that sticketh closer than a brother; but sometimes you want someone you can touch.

My prayer was, "God give me someone who loves You the same as I do." Someone sold out to Christ, who was not playing church, who didn't preach one thing, and live another. God answered my prayer.

During the early years of pastoring, I did a lot of evangelizing. I traveled to many of the states in this United States of America, and to the foreign fields preaching the Gospel of Jesus Christ to dying men and women.

God supplied the need I had to have someone to care for my children and provide my husband with food and nourishment. He did it through the capable hands of Mother Eva Hinton, from Whaleyville, Virginia. Through her I was able to go when God said to go, and be comforted in the fact that she was taking care of them.

Mother has gone on to be with the Lord, but I will always be grateful to her for allowing God to use her in that manner.

One night she invited me to go to Suffolk, Virginia. She discovered that revival was going on, and that Elder James Lewis Moore, from the Tower of Deliverance in Richmond, Virginia, was the preacher. Mother said, "They say he is a good preacher." I prepared myself to go to the revival.

Elder Moore was "a good preacher." The anointing of God rested heavily upon him. As I sat there, it seemed our hearts were knitted together that very night. When he gave the invitation for individuals to come forward to make a commitment to God, he said to me, "My sister, I don't know who you are, but I love the Spirit I feel coming from you. Come up and help me in praying for the needs of the people."

From that night, Elder James Louis Moore has been my friend and brother. You see, none of my brothers were in the Lord at that time, and God gave me one. For twenty-six years and counting, he has been that brother in need. As a woman in ministry, he has been there to help me fight the hard battles that came my way. Praise God!

God has used him many times to speak words of encouragement to me. When I was hurting and needed a friend to talk to in those early years of pastoring, he was there. For years we traveled back and forth to each others' churches to render fellowship services. God would meet us in such a supernatural way. Amen!

His friendship to me is invaluable. I will always thank God for His manservant, who has stayed by my side when others walked away.

I had two of the sweetest people a minister can pastor in my church— Mr. and Mrs. Taylor. We called them "Mom and Papa Taylor." God, in His wisdom, saw fit to call them home, which was a very sad and painful time for me and the members of the church.

Some of the children of Mom and Papa Taylor were members of the St. John's Deliverance Tabernacle in Nyack, New York. They would come down some weekends and be in service with us. When I preached, they would say after the service, "You sound just like our pastor. You are just like her. Both of you preach just alike."

Well! I wanted to meet this lady that I was said to be so much like. As God has it we did meet at the going home service for Papa Taylor. After the service was completed, we went home to comfort and fellowship with the family. I was finally introduced to this great woman of God, Reverend Elizabeth Alston. We sat outside in the yard in the Pughsville section of town, and conversed about the family and the goodness of the Lord.

I was so excited I had finally met a woman pastor who I felt loved God as I did, and who had the same aspirations as I did. It was like meeting myself. I returned back to the church excited about the fact I had met a saint of God. From that day, over twenty years ago, Reverend Elizabeth Alston has been the same as a blood sister to me.

For years we have preached the Gospel together, fasted, prayed, and experienced the supernatural power of God in our relationship. There are many experiences we've had that I am not able to tell you about at this time, but I would like to share this one with one.

We had gone to Rocky Mount, North Carolina, to rest for a few days. During that time of rest, as usual we would get up mornings and get before the Lord in prayer. After we prayed, we would get our Bibles, and if God had spoken to either of us, we would share His word. This was done every day that we were there.

The day came for us to leave. Before we left we desired to go to the religious bookstore that was in town. We checked out of the hotel, and went to the store. While there I could sense the Lord directing us to a certain section of the store and to a particular author. In obedience to the Holy Spirit we purchased the material.

When we were on the highway heading to the Norfolk airport, Pastor Alston began to read (I was driving) one of the books we had purchased. As she read, we began to sense the presence of the Lord in the car. All of a sudden, we felt this person come into the car and sit down between us on the front seat. We could literally feel him sit down. She looked at me and I looked at her as if to say, "Did you feel that?"

The power of God was so great with us at that point, I don't know how I continued to drive, because the tears were streaming down my cheeks. We were giving glory to God, praising Jesus, and it seemed to us that He had sent His angel to join us in that experience. Oh praise God! When I think if it now, His presence is so great with me. My friend, He is real. He wants to reveal Himself to those who are hungry for Him. Just as He manifested Himself to the prophets of old, God wants to reveal Himself to us today. Amen! Male or female, it doesn't matter to God. His call is yet, "Whosoever will, let him come, and let him drink of the water of life freely."

Such a holy presence filled that car. We wept in the presence of the Lord, thanking Him for being so mindful of us. Before we knew anything, we were at the Norfolk airport. After we arrived we were astonished as to what had taken place. He had sent His angel to minister to us.

This is only one of many supernatural experiences we had as we communed together in prayer, yes, and in fasting. The saints would always say to each other, get ready, we know that pastor is coming back fired up, and we did, and we were. It was a retreat with God. This has gone on for years. To God be the glory.

Our ministries have expanded and we don't get the opportunity now to be together, but we thank Him for the times we did have. God has used us to be a source of encouragement and strength to each other.

Bishop Joseph Snead, pastor of the Triumph Pentecostal Church of Deliverance in Newport News, Virginia, and his wife, Naomi, have been friends of mine since I accepted the Lord. Naomi's father, Elder John A. Stephenson, was my first pastor. I thank God for Naomi. She stood by me during those times of crisis that I shared with you earlier. She has always been a true and steady friend. When others looked down upon me, she prayed that the will of God would be done in my life.

In later years, due to ministry, our paths separated, but God in His timing brought us back together in fellowship. We now share in a total way in ministry.

Bishop Snead has been a powerful source of strength for me. He has been a counselor, confidant, and a person of deep compassion. Bishop is a well balanced person. His temperament is that of the Lord—full of compassion. When I would deal with matters in a heated way, he would always show me the better way to deal. I have learned so much from him.

God has reasons for joining certain ones to you. He will give you those who will be a help, and those who will enhance you naturally and spiritually. He has used these friends to instruct, comfort, and encourage me, and yes, also to rebuke me when I was wrong.

Space will not allow me at this time to speak of Bishop James Brinkley, Bishop Paul Thomas, Bishop Emerson Brockington, and many others God used to enrich my life as I labored in the Gospel of Jesus Christ.

Jesus said to those who were following Him, "Verily I say unto you, There is no man that hath left house, or brethren, or sisters, or father, or mother, or wife, or children, or lands, for my sake, and the Gospel's, But he shall receive a hundredfold now in this time, houses, and brethren, and sisters, and mothers, and children, and lands, ... " (Mark 10:29–30)

Whatever you need, God will supply. Let Him choose friends for you. He will never make a mistake. He will give you those who will compliment you, and the call upon your life.

The Vision of the Lord

✞ Chapter 9 ✞

"And it shall come to pass afterward, that I will pour out my spirit upon all flesh; and your sons and your daughters shall prophesy, your old men shall dream dreams, your young men shall see visions."
(Joel 2:28)

In 1986, I went to the World Conference conducted by Morris Cerullo, in Anaheim California. I was there seeking to be refreshed in the Lord, and crying out to know Him. There we heard this great man of God preaching, "That I may know Him and the power of His resurrection, and the fellowship of His suffering, being made conformable unto His death." (Phil.3:10)

You see, this needs to be the cry of every servant of God: to *know* Him; not just to work for Him, but to know Him; to have a personal relationship with Him. The forces of darkness are all around us, and we need to see to it that we have on the whole armor of God so that we may be able to stand against the wiles of the devil.

We don't need to allow ourselves to feel that we are all right and don't need the continual help and strength of God for ministry.

In the vision, I was invited to have dinner with the president. This president was not the president of the United States, but he was a high official of state, or should I say, of the world.

The dinner was held in this large stadium-like building. When I walked inside the building, it was filled with thousands of believers. Some I knew, and some I didn't. It seemed there were levels of seating—an upper and a lower level. Ruby Paige (my personal nurse) was with me.

As I looked around, I had been invited to sit at the table with the president. There were about six others at the table. The people began to talk among themselves about it. I could hear what they were saying, even though I was some distance from them.

Some said, "I don't believe that she is sitting at the table with the president (there was a great distance from some of them to where I was sitting), I'm going to go up and see for myself." They came up to the table, and on the table were name cards, and in front of my seat was one with my name on it.

They did not like it, and began talking again saying, "Who does she think she is to be sitting there? " Oh! It was heartbreaking for me to hear and see how they felt about me.

I got up from the table and started out the door. Evangelist Martha Banks was sitting near the door, and as I made my way to the door she said, "Oh no you're not! You are not going to let what they are saying about you affect you this way." But I was so heartbroken that I could not bear to see and hear the dislike coming to me from the people.

I knew that what had happened was not my doing. I was as surprised as they were. With great pain I left. Ruby was again with me as I walked away. As I walked down the sidewalk, I began to feel badly about leaving. The least I could do was to thank the president for inviting me to the dinner. I said to Ruby, "Let's go back and thank him."

On the way back a gentleman came up to me and said, "I've been commanded to tell you your life will not be the same from this moment on. Your life is going to change. You are going to be blessed with a home [I had a home, but God was planning to give me another, the one I now live in], a car, clothing . . . . [even the type of clothing He was going to give me]."

When I left him, another came up to me from between the cars that were parked on the street, and he said, "I've been listening to the radio broadcast and the messages are great." After him another came and said, "Get busy, you are going to be blessed. Go to those who have and God will touch their hearts to give unto thee." By this time I was so overwhelmed it was as though I could not bear it.

Something woke me out of the vision. When I discovered that I had come out of it, I said to God, "If this is a message for me, please let me go back to sleep and pick it back up." Guess what? He did!

When I went back into the vision, it continued from the last scene. At this time I was near the door of the building and out came the president (he was not there when I left because he had received a telephone call, and he left to take care of it), and he said to me, "Did they tell you that your life will be different from this day forward, that I will touch hearts to give unto thee, that you will be blessed materially?" I said, "Yes!" He said to me, "It shall be. Get in a hurry and do those things that were told to you."

He began to walk away to get into the large limousine that was waiting for him. He turned and said to me, "By the way, is there anyone who's bothering you, or anything that's troubling you that you need me to handle?" I thought about it for a few seconds, and I said to him, "Oh no, what is happening to me is just life; I can deal with it."

A look of astonishment was upon his face—a look of pleasure for the answer I gave him. He then turned and got into the car and left. I turned to Ruby and said, "What in the world is this? What is going on?" We walked away down the sidewalk from the building. My attention was drawn in the vision to Ruby as she walked with me. Our steps were synchronized. Ruby had a limp, but she was totally in step with me, and from that scene, I came out of the vision.

God has made me know what this vision meant. When God has placed His hands upon you to do a work for Him, regardless of what people think, feel, or say, He will perform it. Also, everyone is not going to rejoice with you when you are called by God. Doth this make the Word of God be of none effect, God forbid!

Some will not like it, especially if you are a female. There will be those who will not agree with it. Their unbelief and jealousy will be so strong that if you are not careful, you will be so hurt or frustrated, you will let go and walk away from His will for your life.

God has our lives planned. Even before we were born, He has chosen the path for us to trod, and in obedience to Him, we must follow in spite of what man (mankind) says or thinks.

Thanks be to God for His Holy Spirit in you that will minister to your heart and mind, and will bring you into agreement with Him. Don't allow the dislike of others, their traditions, or their beliefs, to cause you to miss God. Don't allow the pain to dictate your actions.

When you have a relationship with Him, and you know His voice, you must obey Him. He knew you from the foundation of the world, and called and anointed you to do His will. Obey Him, and He will fight for you. The glory of the Lord will be revealed and all flesh shall see it together: for the mouth of the Lord hath spoken it. (Isa. 40:5)